# Tyneham
### with Worbarrow

# Then & Now

**Tyneham with Worbarrow Then & Now**

Copyright © Gordon Lewis 2016

All rights reserved. No part of this book may be reproduced in any form or by any electronic or mechanical means, including storage and retrieval systems, without permission in writing from the author, except by a reviewer who may quote passages in a review.

ISBN 978-1539706946

# Tyneham
**with Worbarrow**

# Then & Now

Gordon Lewis

**Other titles by Gordon Lewis**

***Limb and Blood – the story of a Wiltshire family***
(Bedeguar Books 1995)

***Dolly's Imber*** *(Revised Edition)*
(Rebbeck Cards/Createspace Publishing 2015)

***Imber Then & Now***
(Createspace Publishing 2015)

# Introduction

Located in an ancient valley close to Dorset's Jurassic coast the people of Tyneham and nearby Worbarrow had lived in their stone cottages without too much interference from the outside world. That would change forever during November 1943 when a notice to evacuate the area was issued by Southern Command acting on the instructions of the British Government.

No doubt the villagers may have heard rumours of something similar happening to the inhabitants of Imber, located in the middle of Wiltshire's Salisbury Plain, just two weeks earlier, but no one had expected a second English village to be taken over as part of the war effort so soon after another.

Whereas the people of Imber were given 47 days to leave their homes, Tyneham residents were provided with just 33 days in which to vacate. Unlike the situation at Imber where families were forced to find their own alternative accommodation without assistance, Southern Command promised that "everything possible will be done to help you, both by payment of compensation, and by finding other accommodation for you".

One common theme that existed between Imber and Tyneham was that the villagers in both communities expected to return after the cessation of hostilities, but it was not to be. The War Office already owned most of Imber and, in 1948, the British Army issued a compulsory purchase on all properties within the parish of Tyneham.

This move was not without protest and the Tyneham Action Group was formed in 1968 prompting Edward Heath, the Prime Minister at that time, to set up the Defence Lands Committee. Chaired by Lord Nugent of Guildford, the committee was instructed to explore the possibility of restoring requisitioned lands back to private ownership.

The subsequent report, published in 1973, proposed that the Lulworth Ranges, of which Tyneham and Worbarrow were an integral part, could be released from the Ministry of Defence, with any strategic operations relocated to Wales.  This proposal was quickly rejected by the Welsh authorities, while Dorset County Council suggested that any demilitarisation of the area would result in significant damage to the local economy.  It was decided, therefore, that the ranges would remain under military control.

Today Tyneham and Worbarrow are accessible most weekends as well as during the month of August, although military operations continue to take precedence over visiting tourists.  Ruined cottages stand in tribute to the sacrifice of former inhabitants, while St. Mary's Church, the School and Tyneham Farm preserve the history of an almost forgotten community.

When I first visited Tyneham several years ago I was struck by its similarities with Imber, where members of my own family had once lived.  I may not know the names or recognise the faces of those who once called Tyneham home but, having completed detailed research, I can now identify with them through this pictorial record of **Tyneham with Worbarrow Then & Now**.

*Gordon Lewis*
*October 2016*

# Village Map

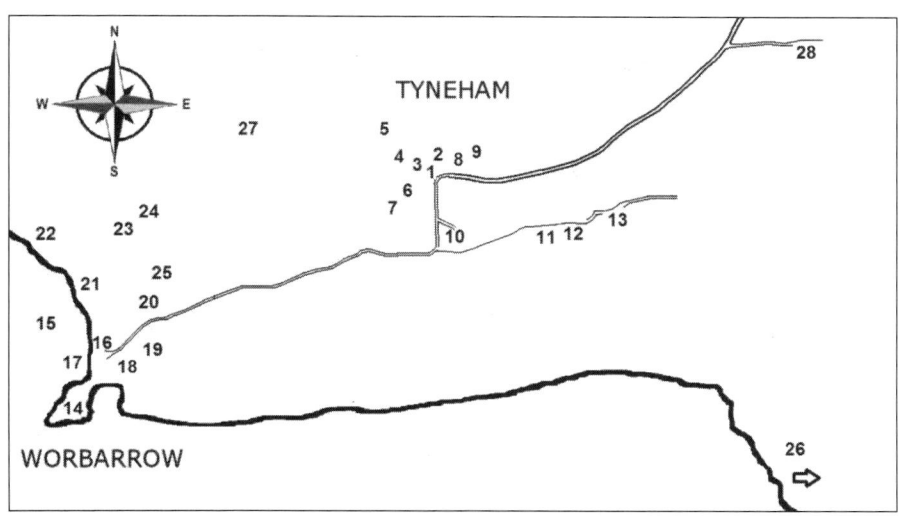

- 1 Post Office Row
- 2 St. Mary's Church
- 3 Village School
- 4 Rectory Cottages
- 5 The Rectory
- 6 Laundry Cottages
- 7 Gwyle Cottages
- 8 Double Cottages
- 9 Gould's Cottage
- 10 Tyneham Farm
- 11 Gardener's Cottage
- 12 Village Hall
- 13 Tyneham House
- 14 Worbarrow Tout
- 15 Worbarrow Bay
- 16 Sea Cottage
- 17 Worbarrow Beach
- 18 Coastguard Station
- 19 Hill Cottage
- 20 Gatekeeper's Cottage
- 21 Sheepleaze
- 22 The Bungalow
- 23 Minterne's Cottage
- 24 Fern Hollow
- 25 Rose Cottage
- 26 South Egliston Farm
- 27 Baltington Farm
- 28 North Egliston Farm

# Safety Guidelines

Although much of Tyneham and Worbarrow is accessible during opening times, other areas are strictly out of bounds to the general public. Trespassers risk arrest, prosecution and injury. At all times please keep to the metalled or gravelled roads and observe all visible signs.

**DISCLAIMER**

Although every attempt has been made to match historic images with exact locations, neither the author nor the publisher will be held responsible for any errors or omissions, including those that may be the result of access restrictions imposed by the Ministry of Defence.

# Tyneham

**In this small rural village on Dorset's Jurassic coast
There now only remains aged spirits and ghosts
For the war effort, Tyneham played its part
For our great nation, Tyneham gave its heart**

Taken from *The Tale of Tyneham* by Angela Whybrow

# Post Office Row

Post Office Row with its telephone kiosk was once described as the gateway to Tyneham village and was the scene that greeted inhabitants and visitors on a daily basis.

# Post Office Row

Apart from its derelict cottages, Post Office Row is easily identified today with its replica telephone kiosk reminding visitors of a forgotten era.

# Post Office Row

Post Office Row provided homes for the local shepherd, the school mistress and, as the name suggests, the sub-post mistress. The telephone kiosk arrived sometime between 1920 and 1930 when these two photographs were taken.

# Post Office Row

As recent as the late-1970s, crumbling roofs were still visible on the cottages of Post Office Row. Today the chimney stacks and much of the upper walls have completely disappeared.

# Post Office Row

Another view of Post Office Row with some of its former inhabitants standing outside their Tyneham homes. It is an idyllic scene which contrasts with the dereliction that greets visitors to the village today.

# St. Mary's Church

At the heart of the village lies the parish church of St. Mary which is one of only a handful of original buildings to remain. Dating from the 13th century, the south transept was rebuilt during the mid-1800s.

# St. Mary's Church

A second view of Tyneham church features a locally made signpost situated between the church steps and the parish tap, which was consecrated in 1853. Today the tap remains, although it is many years since it was last used.

# Altar Window

Tyneham church boasts a number of original stained glass windows, including the altar window depicting St. Mary and the infant Christ. It is dedicated to the memory of Grace Draper (1874-1923) of Middlesex who, with her barrister husband, had a second home at nearby Worbarrow.

# The Chancel

Considered to be the most sacred part of any Christian church, this rare photograph depicts the chancel and altar of St. Mary's Church, Tyneham before the evacuation.

# The Chancel

Today the chancel remains the focal point of St. Mary's Church which now serves as an exhibition centre detailing the history of Tyneham village and its former residents.

# Church Organ

Following the evacuation of Tyneham, the church organ was moved from the chancel of St. Mary's to the neighbouring parish church of Steeple. The church bells also found a new home in the same village.

# Church Organ

The organ may no longer be played at Tyneham, but its location is still visible and the architecture remains the same as it was when the organ would have been installed.

# Village School

Tyneham Elementary School was built in 1856 and was designed to accommodate 60 children. After the Coastguard Station at Worbarrow was shut down in 1912, numbers fell and the school itself was closed in 1932 when the building became the village hall.

# Village School

The original village hall was a wooden structure located next to Gardener's Cottage, whereas the school was a much more substantial stone building. Today the school has been used to recreate a Victorian classroom.

# Village Tap

More than seventy years after Tyneham was evacuated the Biblical inscription on the village tap still promises the gift of water, although a nearby and more recent sign warns "Do Not Drink"!

# Rectory Cottages

Facing St. Mary's Church and the village school is a row of dwellings known as Rectory Cottages which originally served as the Rectory. After the new Rectory was built in 1853, the property was divided into several smaller homes.

# The Rectory

Built halfway through the 19th century and 90 years before Tyneham was evacuated, the Rectory provided a wealth of luxurious rooms that were connected by a maze of corridors.

# The Rectory

Following a mysterious fire in the 1960s, which many believe was a deliberate arson attack, the Rectory was reduced to a single storey and is no longer accessible due to safety concerns.

# The Rectory

The main entrance to the Rectory serves as a reminder of a once impressive building, although what appears to be the signs of target practice are clearly visible on either side of the doorway.

# The Rectory

The Rectory had an extensive range of outbuildings that were once used for storage but also acted as stables. The last vicar to live at Tyneham used to keep his motor car behind the large double doors.

# Laundry Cottages

This row of cottages takes its name from the occupation of one of its inhabitants. Harriet Taylor, assisted by her sister Helen, provided a laundry service for the occupants of Tyneham House as well as other villagers.

# Gwyle Cottages

One of these semi-detached properties, together known as Gwyle Cottages after the nearby river which flows to Worbarrow, provided a home to the family of Henry Grant who worked as a woodman in the local area.

# Double Cottages

Nestled below North Hill is a pair of dwellings that have become known as Double Cottages. With open farmland on either side, this would have provided a near-idyllic location for any family to live.

# Double Cottages

An alternative view of Double Cottages revealing how little remains today. At the time of the evacuation, George Everett and his family resided in one of these cottages, while Henry Hawkins lived next door.

# Gould's Cottage

A short distance from Double Cottages is a property that has been incorrectly identified in recent years as Gardener's Cottage. In fact, this was the home of Thomas Gould from whom the large cottage takes its name.

# Tyneham Farm

One of several farms located in the parish of Tyneham, only the foundations remain of the original farmhouse which was last occupied by Walter Smith and his housekeeper, Kathleen Bristowe.

# Tyneham Farm

Another view of Tyneham Farmhouse looking towards Worbarrow. Visitors may be surprised to realise that one of the farm's remaining outbuildings, once used as a cart shed, is now preserved as a public convenience!

# Tyneham Farm

Although Tyneham Farm's Great Barn has been partially restored in recent years, including a new corrugated roof, the building is instantly recognisable more than 70 years after it was last used as part of a busy farming community.

# Tyneham Farm

Like all farms across the country, Tyneham Farm was a vibrant place to be, providing employment for many people living in the village. Today the remaining buildings contain vintage agricultural machinery from a bygone era.

# Tyneham Farm

Also recognisable is the farmyard which has undergone significant restoration in recent years. The grain store and adjoining stables now contain a rural exhibition that recalls something of Tyneham's farming past.

# Gardener's Cottage

Identified as Gardener's Cottage on Ordnance Survey maps dating from the late 19th century, others have suggested it was Coachman's Cottage. By 1939 it was known as Tyneham House Cottage and was occupied by a gardener!

# Village Hall

A wooden village hall once stood adjacent to Gardener's Cottage until the 1930s when, after the closure of the village school, the community facility found a new home in the old school building.

# Tyneham House

Tyneham House was once considered to be the jewel in Dorset's countryside, combining a traditionally styled manor house with tree-lined avenues and landscaped gardens.

# Tyneham House

With 14th century origins, Tyneham House was re-modelled during the reign of Queen Elizabeth I and became known as a fine example of Tudor architecture. After 1943 its destruction was reputedly hastened by the War Office.

# Tyneham House

A closer view of Tyneham House reveals an Elizabethan style building which was typical of manor houses across England during the 16$^{th}$ century. Its demolition can only be described as a crime against history.

# Tyneham House

An alternative view of Tyneham House taken from the north. Now obstructed by almost a century of tree growth, it is only the sunlight shining through empty windows that serves as a reminder to this once great house.

# Medieval Hall

One of Tyneham's hidden secrets is the 14th century hall which was originally built by the Russell family. It was incorporated into the Elizabethan house 200 years later.

# Medieval Hall

Today the Medieval Hall survives in an amazing state of preservation when compared to the adjoining Tyneham House. Inside are some fine examples of 14$^{th}$ century timber frames, but these are not accessible to the public.

# Estate Buildings

Like many English country estates, Tyneham House was surrounded by a diverse range of outbuildings, many of which have survived despite the entire area being taken over by the War Office in 1943.

# Estate Buildings

In addition to the usual stables and coach houses, Tyneham House also boasted its own underground reservoir as well as a Brew House, the remains of which are shown below.

# Worbarrow Tout

The coastal hamlet of Worbarrow was once a busy fishing community like so many settlements located along Dorset's Jurassic coastline. Worbarrow Tout, an old word for "look out", is situated at the eastern end of the bay.

# Worbarrow Tout

Another view of Worbarrow Tout with Sea Cottage visible in the foreground. Despite its idyllic location, the cottage was constantly bombarded by winter storms coming off the English Channel.

# Worbarrow Bay

# Worbarrow Bay

With and without the presence of Sea Cottage (opposite), Worbarrow Bay remains a stunning example of Dorset's geological heritage.

# Sea Cottage

Sea Cottage was home to generations of local fishermen who would sail into the bay and beyond to catch their precious cargo. Second only to farming, fishing was one of the main industries supporting Tyneham and Worbarrow.

# Worbarrow Beach

Worbarrow Beach has always been a popular destination, as this early photograph shows. Sea Cottage is a prominent feature while a Victorian bathing machine provides modesty for those wishing to swim in the sea.

# Coastguard Station

Until 1912 Worbarrow boasted its own Coastguard Station which also helped to swell the local population. Its closure and subsequent demolition attributed to the eventual demise of Tyneham School 20 years later.

# Hill Cottage

Located behind the Coastguard Station was Hill Cottage, which was home to generations of the same family until the evacuation in 1943. Although little remains of the original building, the view is still as stunning as ever.

# Gatekeeper's Cottage

Located opposite Hill Cottage and one of the first buildings seen when walking from Tyneham to Worbarrow, Gatekeeper's Cottage has sometimes been referred to as Gate Cottage and may have once served as a toll house.

# Sheepleaze

During 1910 permission was given to Warwick Draper, a Middlesex Barrister, to build a house on the clifftop overlooking Worbarrow Bay. Occupied during the summer months, it was a second home for the Draper family.

# The Bungalow

Ten years after the construction of Sheepleaze, a second property was built further along the clifftop. It was home to the widow of a cotton magnate from the Midlands and, after her death in 1933, was used as a holiday home.

# Minterne's Cottage

A short distance inland from the Bungalow was the home of the Minterne family from whom the property took its name. The occupants ran a small holding which kept the local community supplied with milk, butter and eggs.

# Fern Hollow

Across the stream from Minterne's Cottage was Fern Hollow which was one of the few brick built houses in the area. Although traces of the foundations remain, there is very little left to indicate the presence of this property.

# Rose Cottage

In a long forgotten location below Gatekeeper's Cottage, the idyllically named Rose Cottage has now been reclaimed by nature. Those walking along the clifftop path can sometimes glimpse the one remaining chimney.

# South Egliston Farm

East of Worbarrow was the thatched farmhouse of South Egliston. Like Rose Cottage, nature has reclaimed much of this property which was one of several farms in the Tyneham area.

# Baltington Farm

The higher trackway connecting Worbarrow with Tyneham passes the now abandoned Baltington Farm. There is little to see of the original farmhouse, although many of the farm buildings are still visible.

# Baltington Farm

The pond has long since evaporated, but it is reputed that the ghost of Jane Gilbert, a dairymaid who committed suicide by hanging herself in the cowshed, still haunts the area surrounding Baltington Farm.

# North Egliston Farm

As the road rises from Tyneham towards Corfe Castle, North Egliston Farm can be seen in the distance. The traditional English farmyard is still surrounded by the former farmhouse and outbuildings.

# North Egliston Farm

Compared to many other buildings in the area, North Egliston Farm has survived better than some. Although former homes have become empty shells, the roofs have remained surprisingly complete.

# Tyneham Lament

Born at Fryern Court, Fordingbridge, Hampshire, Lilian Bond spent much of her early life living at Tyneham House which had been purchased by her ancestor in 1683. Her words, displayed within Tyneham Farm's Great Barn, speak for all who were evacuated from the village in 1943.

I shall not see your blinded face
Dear house now crumbling into dust
I will not gaze upon your death
Who gave me life to hold in trust

Your kindly hearthstone has grown cold
Yet silently your faith you keep
Mute victim of the strife of men
With generations long asleep

**Lilian Bond 1887-1980**

**Bibliography:**

BOND, Lilian, *Tyneham: A Lost Heritage* (Wimborne, The Dovecote Press, 1984)

BUCKTON, Henry, *The Lost Villages: In Search of Britain's Vanished Communities* (London, I B Tauris & Co. Ltd, 2008)

LEGG, Rodney, *Tyneham Ghost Village* (Wincanton, Dorset Publishing Company, 1998)

**Picture Credits:**

**Ann Hollyoake**; back cover

**Copyright Control**; front cover (secondary), pages 10, 12 (top and bottom), 14 (top), 15 (top), 16 (top), 18, 20, 22 (top), 25 (top), 26 (top), 27 (top), 29 (top), 30 (top), 31 (top), 32 (top), 33 (top), 34 (top), 35 (top), 36 (top), 37 (top), 38 (top), 39 (top), 40 (top), 41 (top), 42 (top), 43 (top), 44 (top), 45 (top), 46, 48 (top), 50 (top), 51 (top), 52, 54 (top), 55 (top), 56 (top), 57 (top), 58 (top), 59 (top), 60 (top), 61 (top), 62 (top), 63 (top), 64 (top), 65 (top), 66 (top), 67 (top), 68 (top)

**Gordon Lewis**; front cover (main), pages 9, 11, 13 (bottom), 14 (bottom), 15 (bottom), 16 (bottom), 17, 19, 21, 22 (bottom), 23 (top and bottom), 24, 25 (bottom), 26 (bottom), 27 (bottom), 28, 29 (bottom), 30 (bottom), 31 (bottom), 32 (bottom), 33 (bottom), 34 (bottom), 35 (bottom), 36 (bottom), 37 (bottom), 38 (bottom), 39 (bottom), 40 (bottom), 41 (bottom), 42 (bottom), 43 (bottom), 44 (bottom), 45 (bottom), 47, 48 (bottom), 49 (top and bottom), 50 (bottom), 51 (bottom), 53, 54 (bottom), 55 (bottom), 56 (bottom), 57 (bottom), 58 (bottom), 59 (bottom), 60 (bottom), 61 (bottom), 62 (bottom), 63 (bottom), 65 (bottom), 66 (bottom), 67 (bottom), 68 (bottom), 69

**Ryhope Ranger**; pages 64 (bottom)

**Southern Newspapers**; pages 13 (top)

Printed in Great Britain
by Amazon